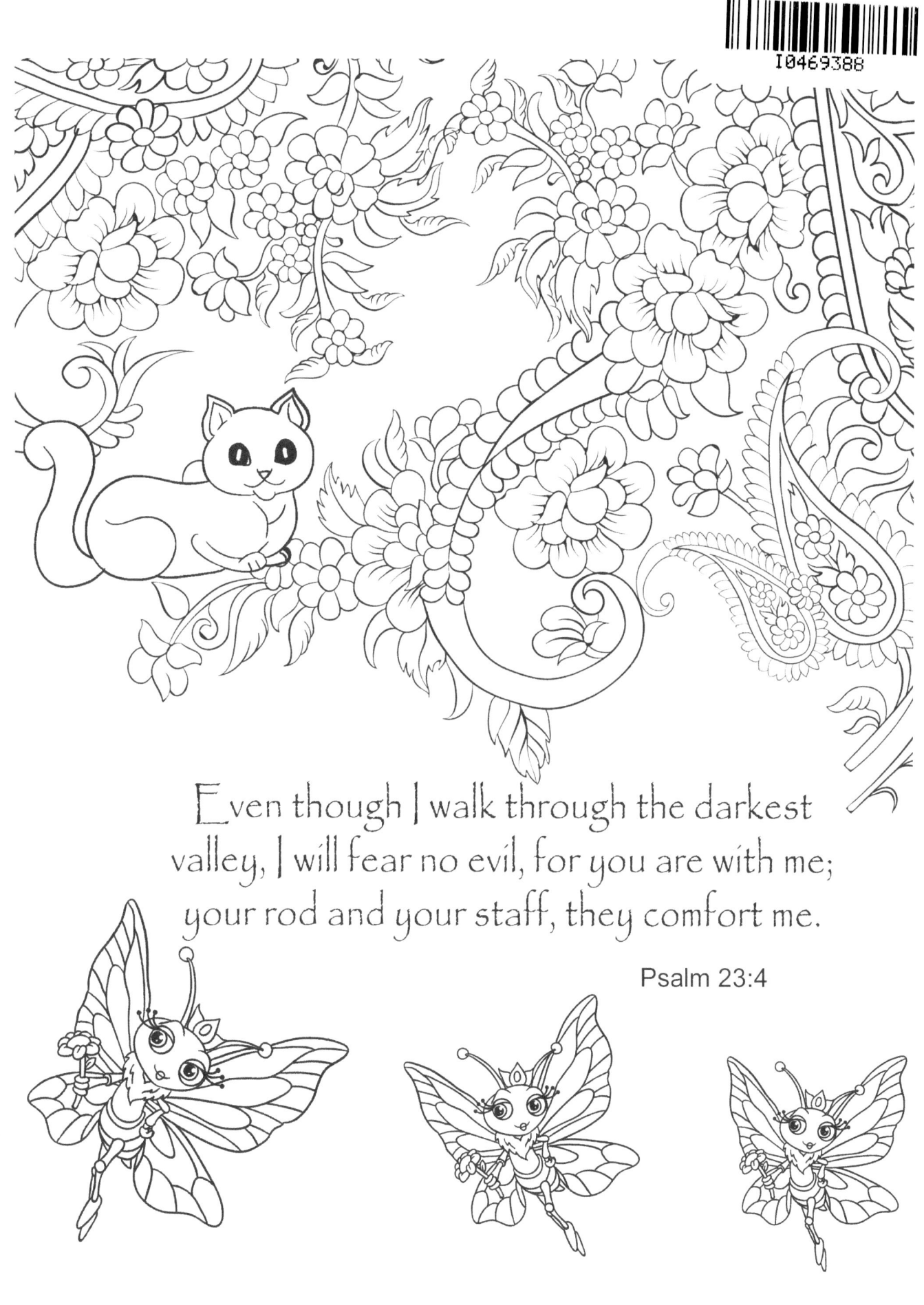

Even though I walk through the darkest valley, I will fear no evil, for you are with me; your rod and your staff, they comfort me.

Psalm 23:4

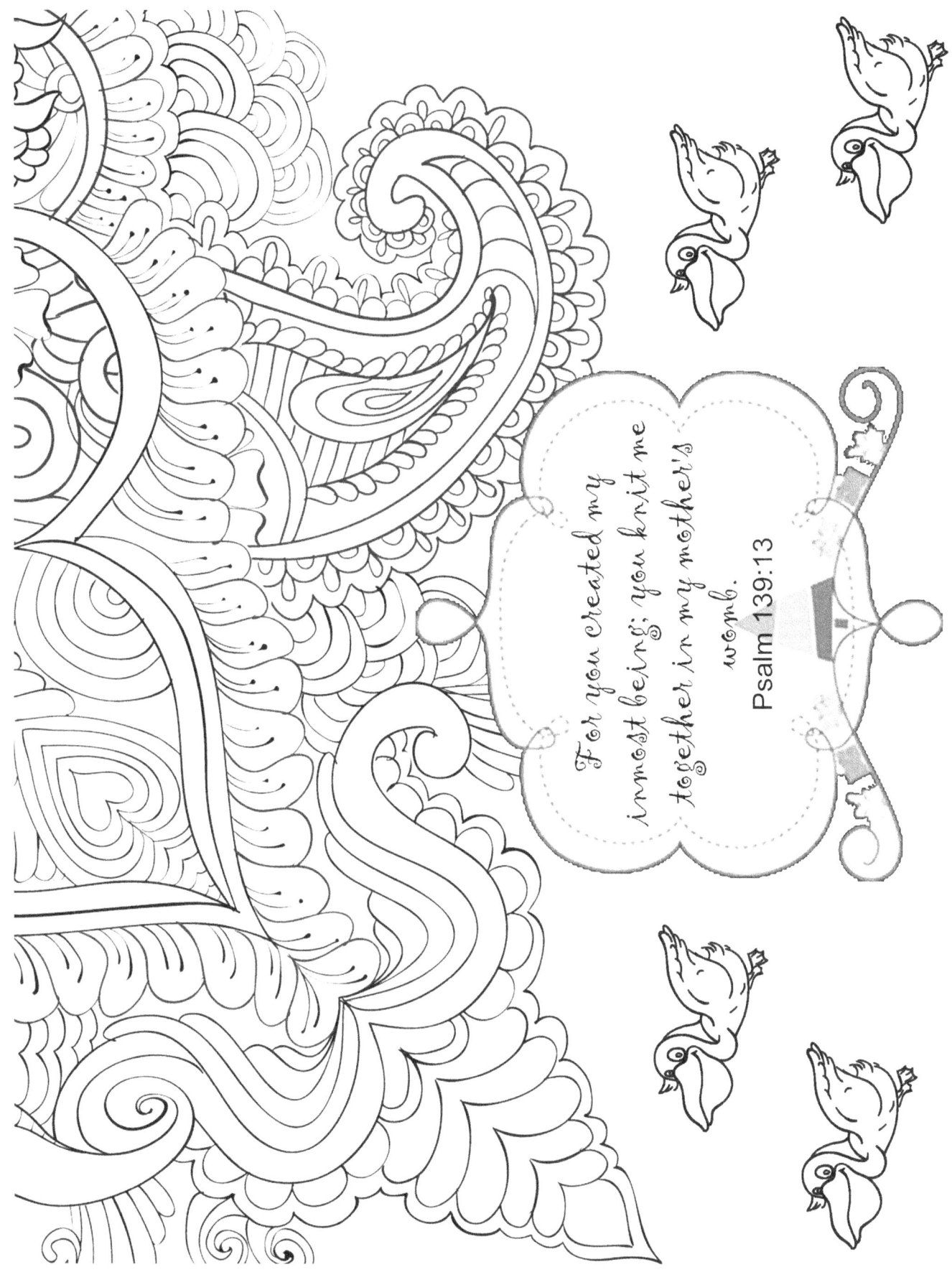

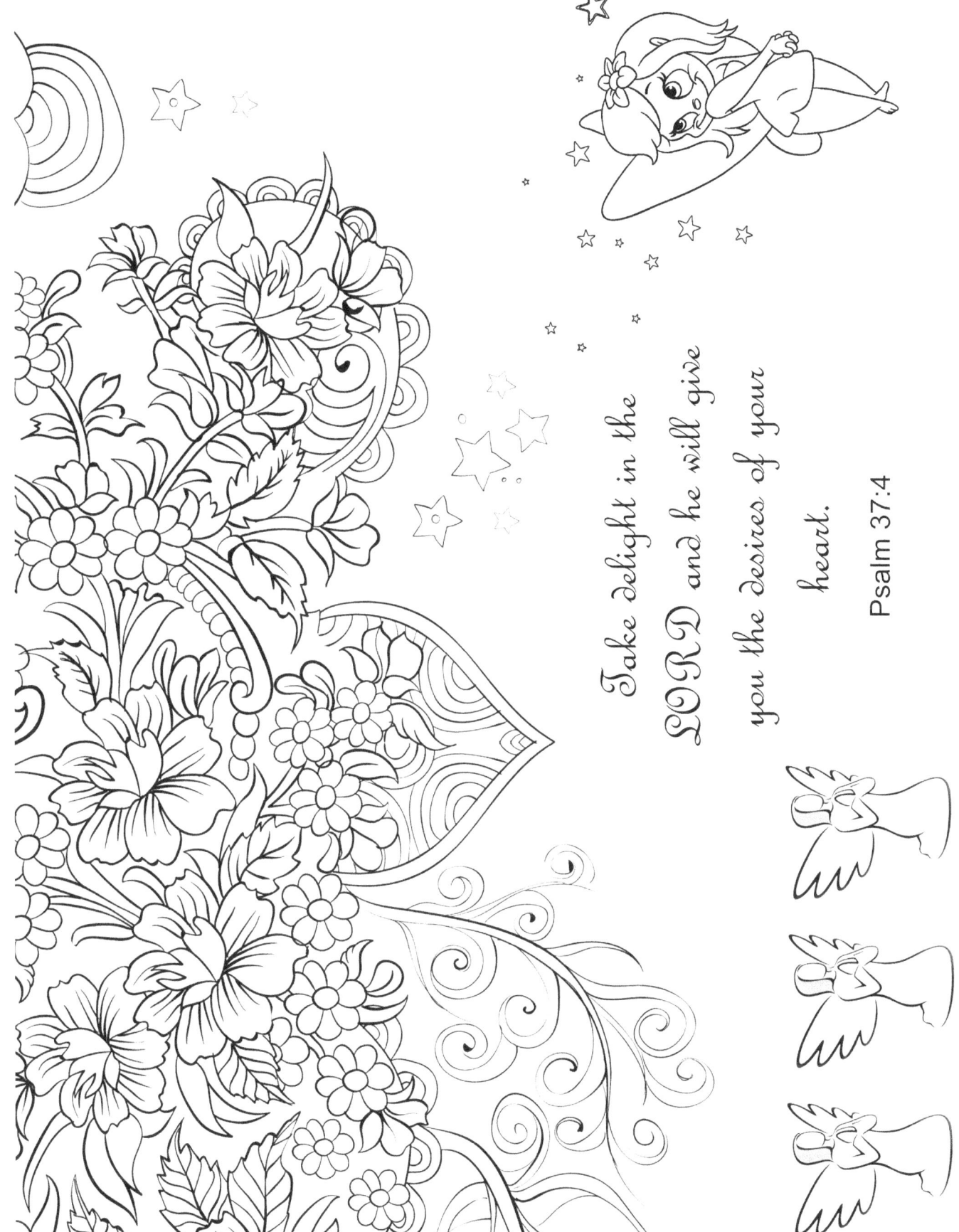

Take delight in the LORD and he will give you the desires of your heart.

Psalm 37:4

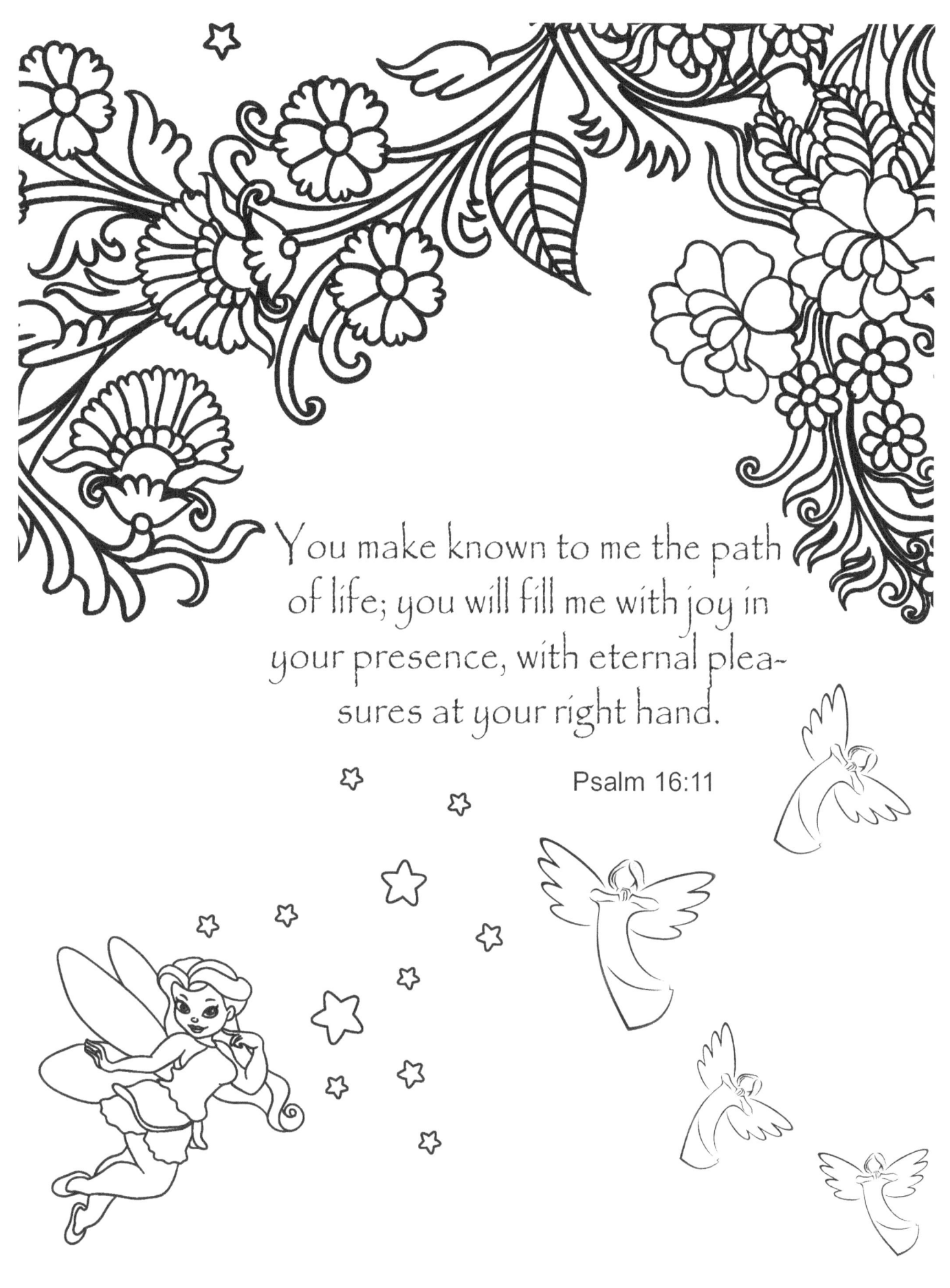

You make known to me the path of life; you will fill me with joy in your presence, with eternal pleasures at your right hand.

Psalm 16:11

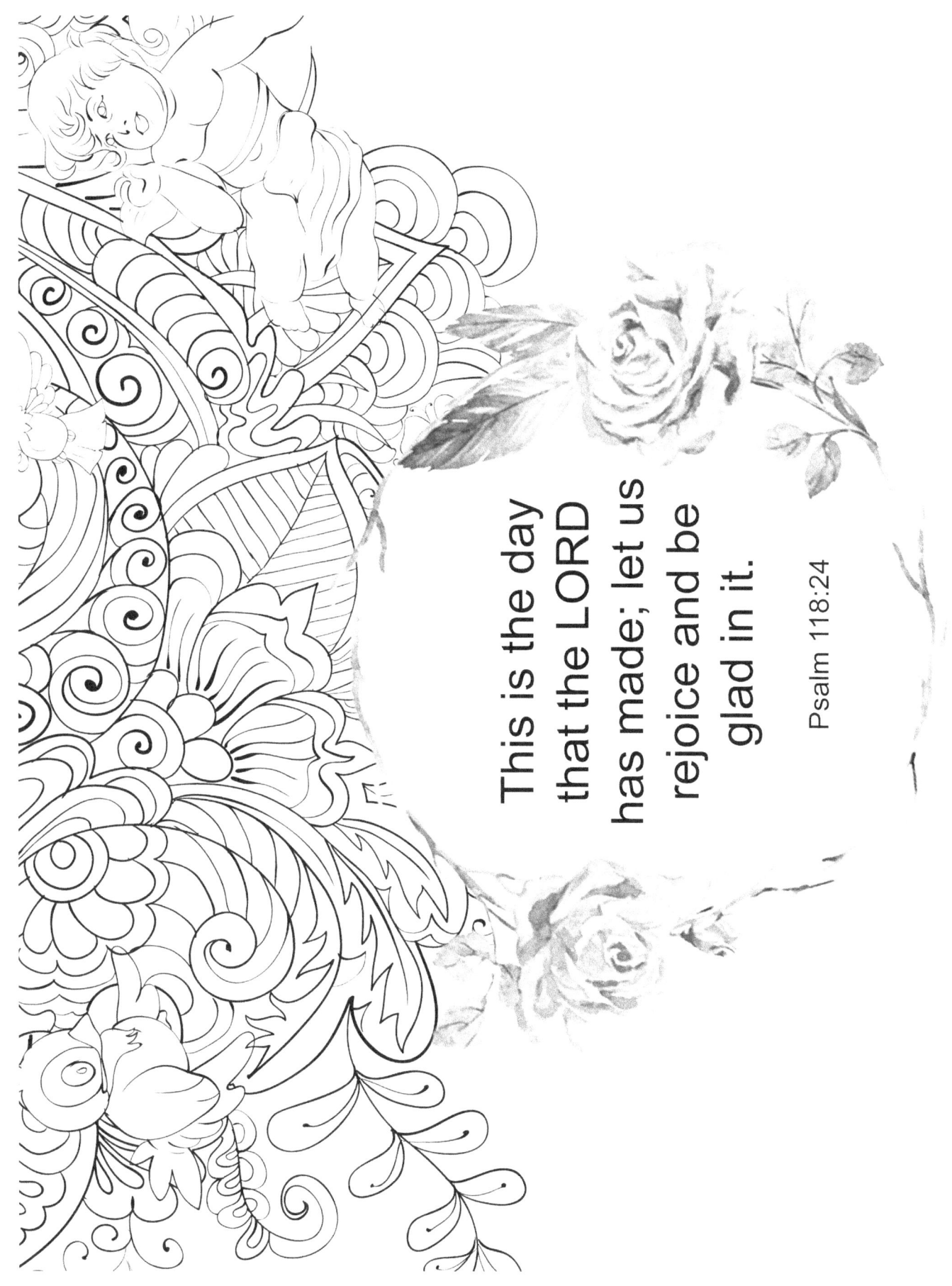

This is the day
that the LORD
has made; let us
rejoice and be
glad in it.

Psalm 118:24

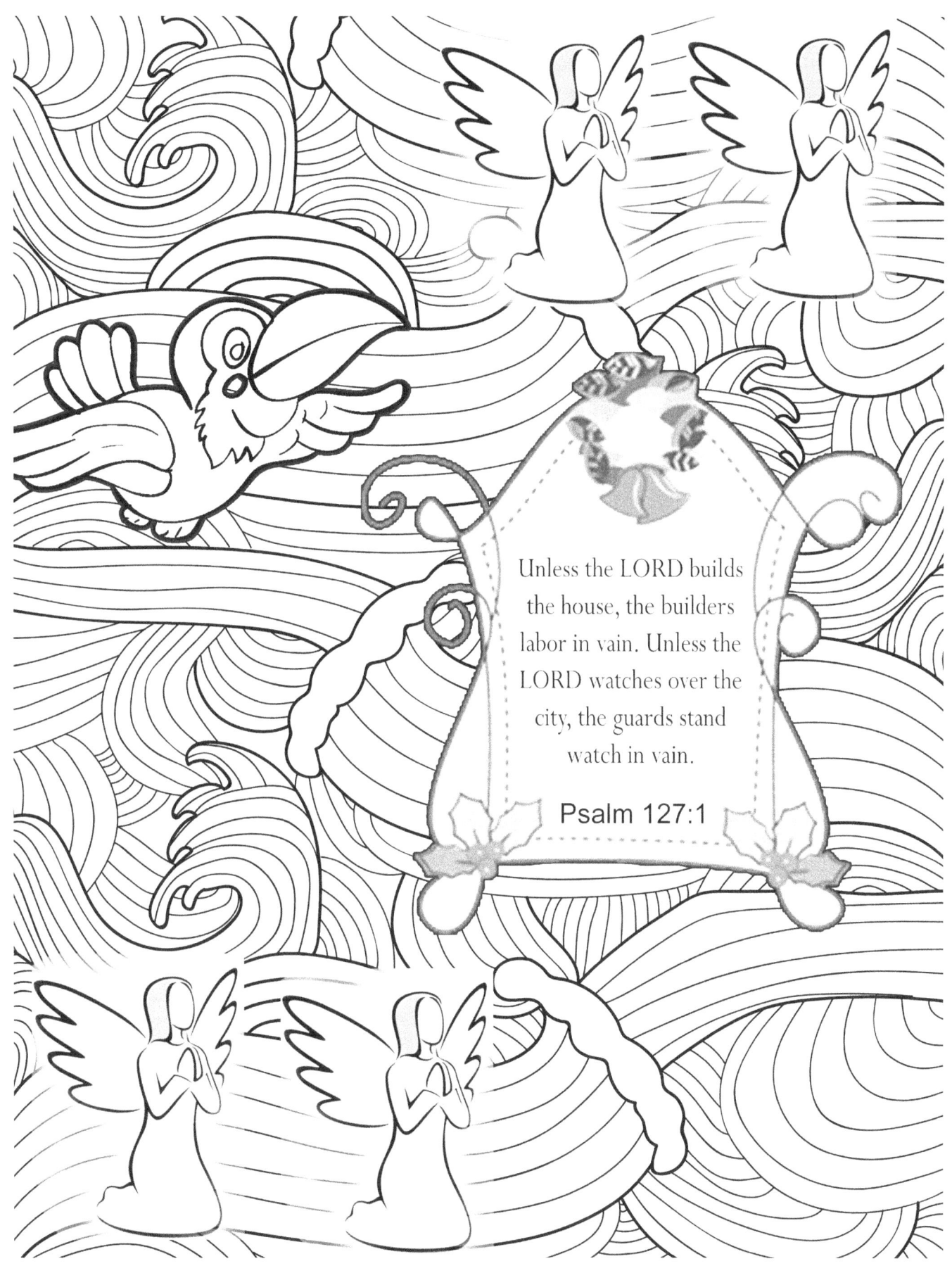

Unless the LORD builds the house, the builders labor in vain. Unless the LORD watches over the city, the guards stand watch in vain.

Psalm 127:1

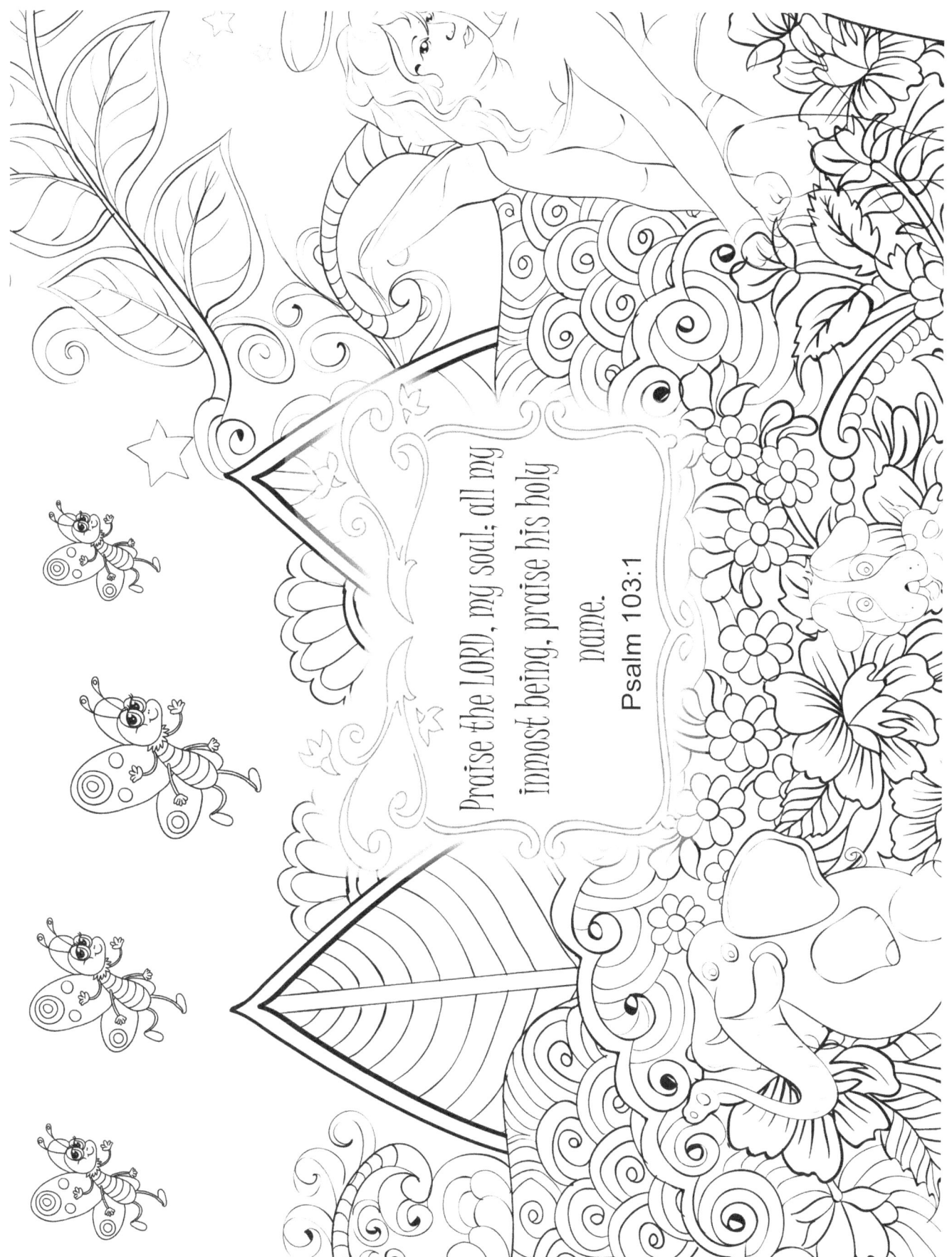

Praise the LORD, my soul; all my
inmost being, praise his holy
name. Psalm 103:1

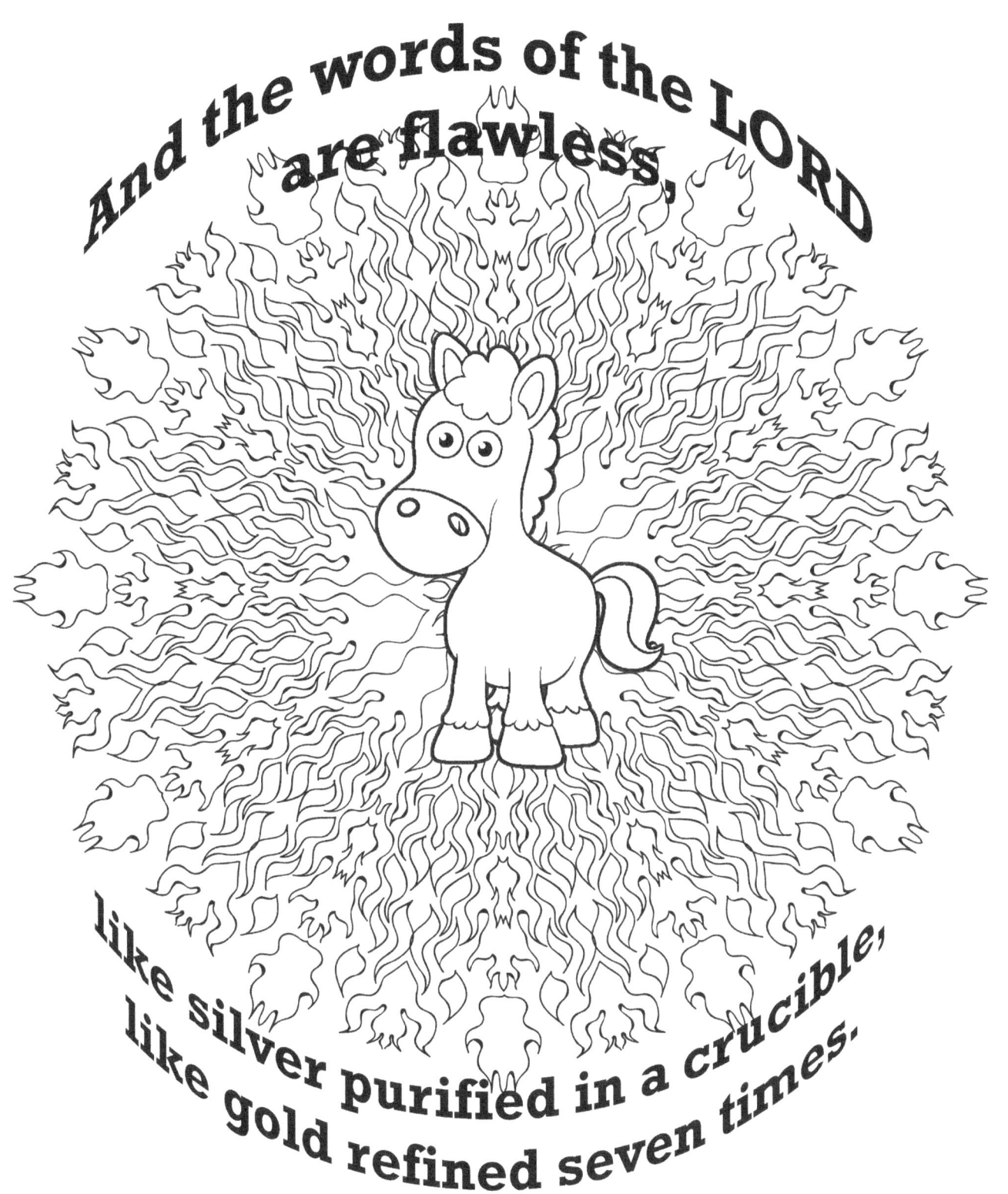

And the words of the LORD are flawless,

like silver purified in a crucible,
like gold refined seven times.

Psalm 12:6

Be still, and know that I am God. I will be exalted among the nations,

I will be exalted in the earth!   Psalm 46:10

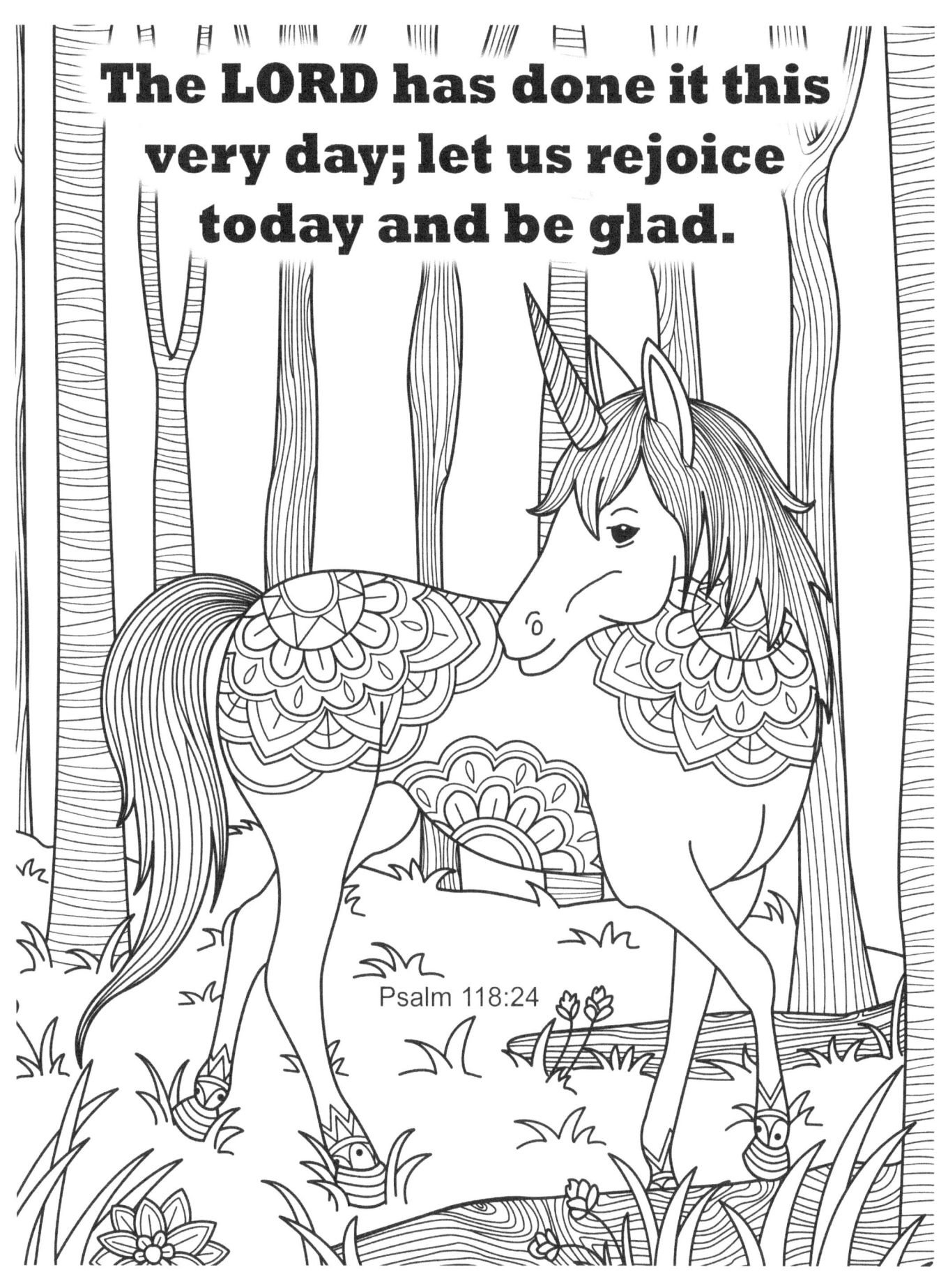

The LORD has done it this very day; let us rejoice today and be glad.

Psalm 118:24

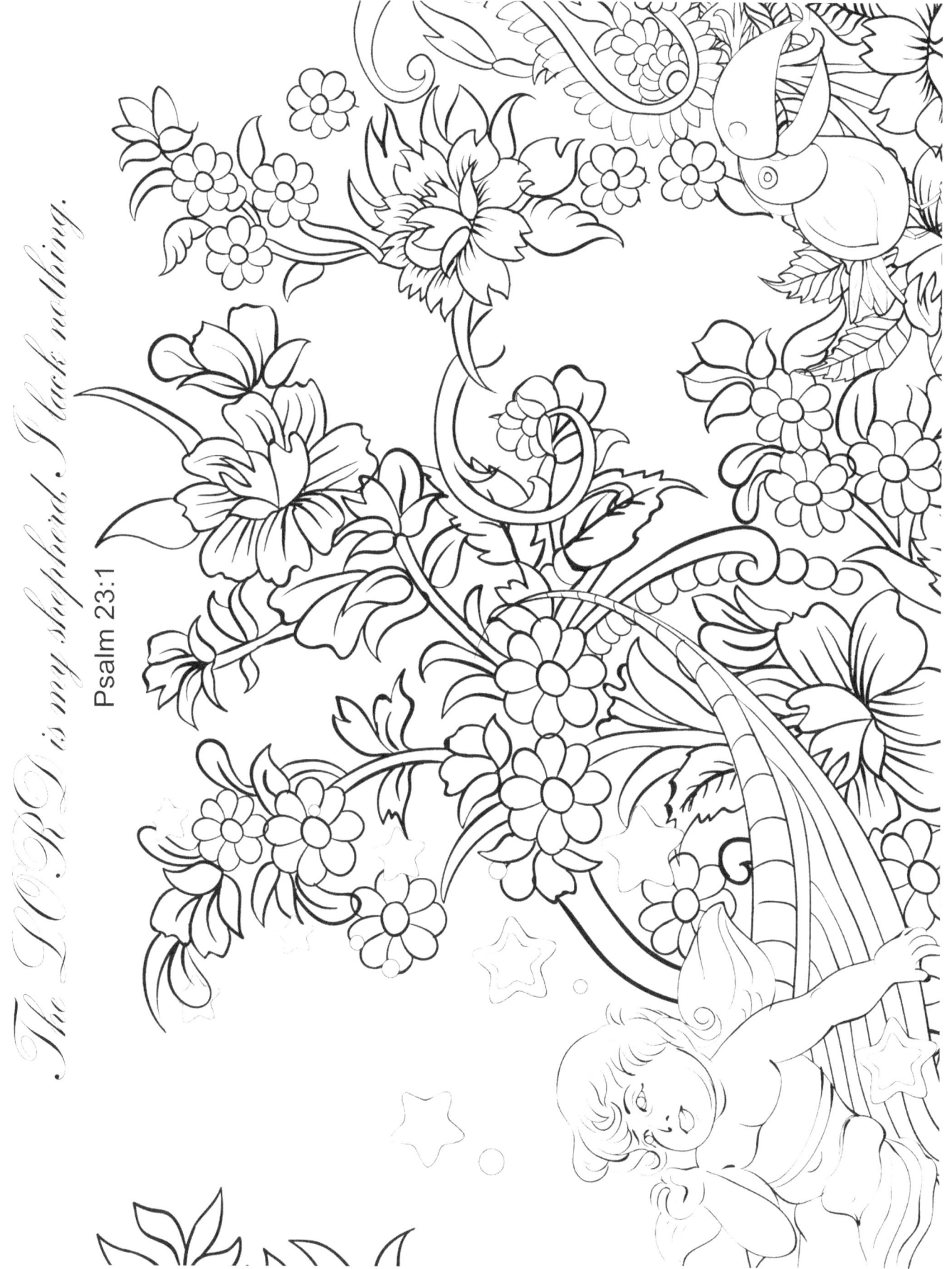

The LORD is my shepherd, I lack nothing.

Psalm 23:1

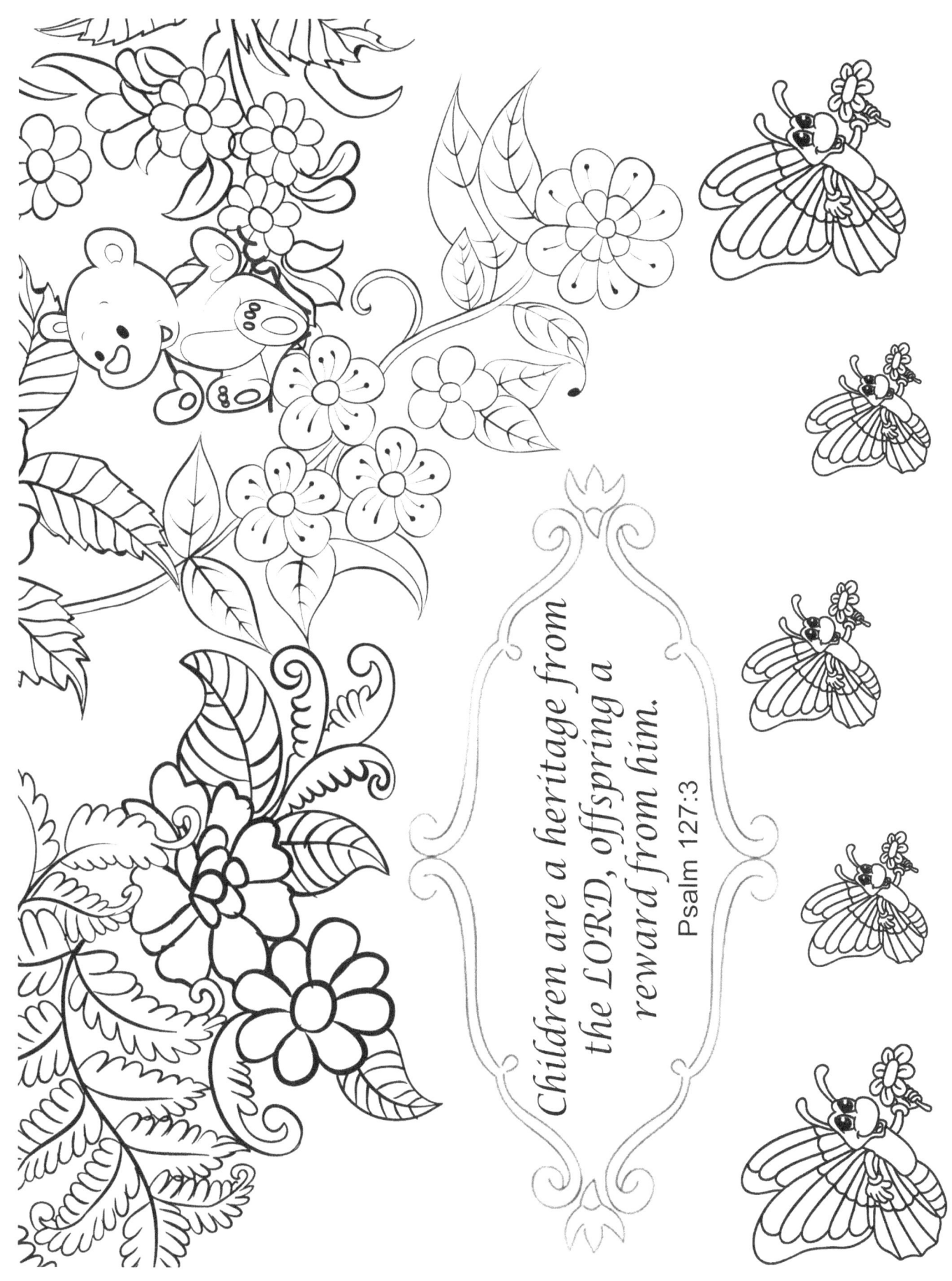

Children are a heritage from the LORD, offspring a reward from him.

Psalm 127:3

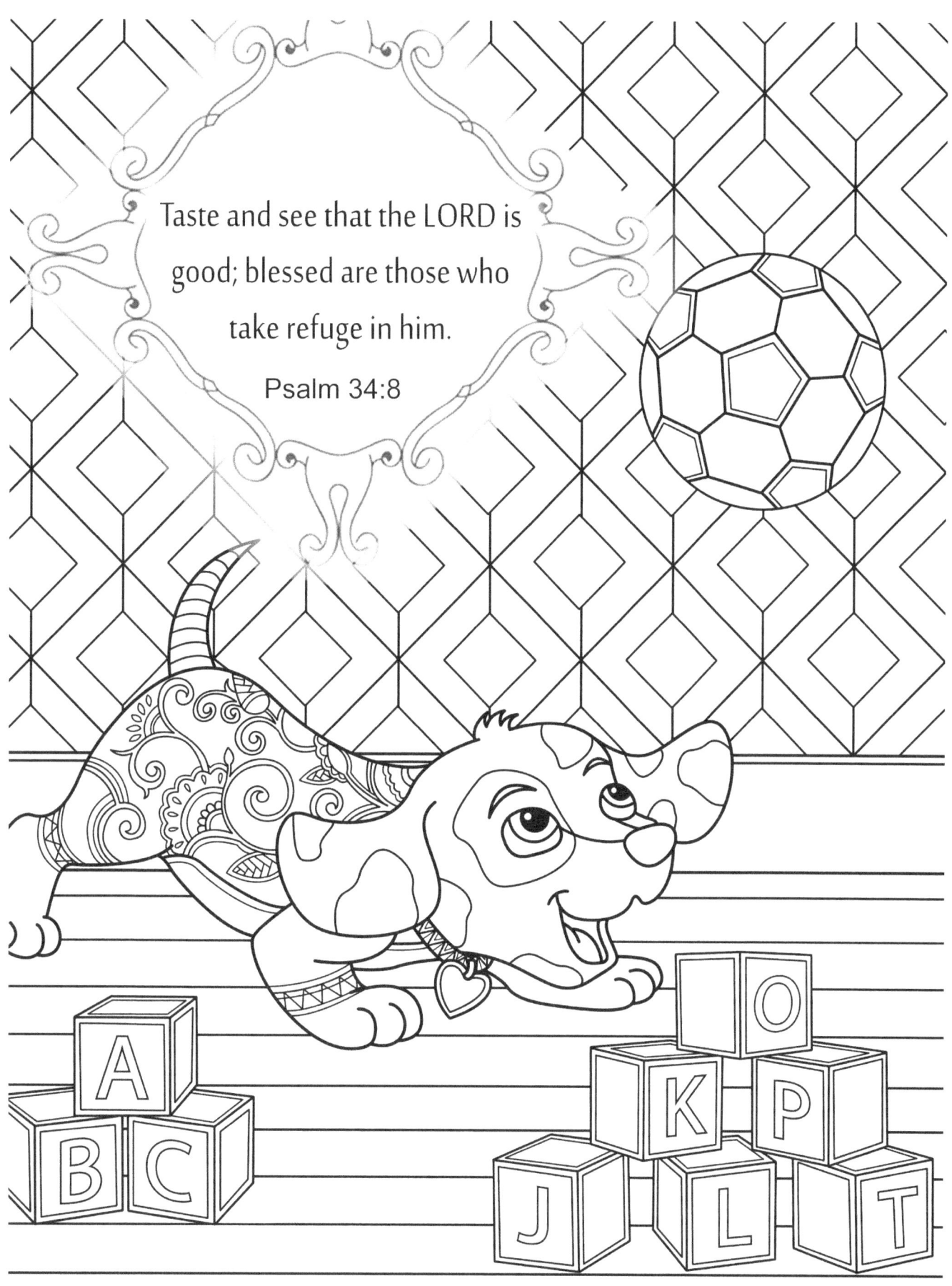

Taste and see that the LORD is good; blessed are those who take refuge in him.

Psalm 34:8

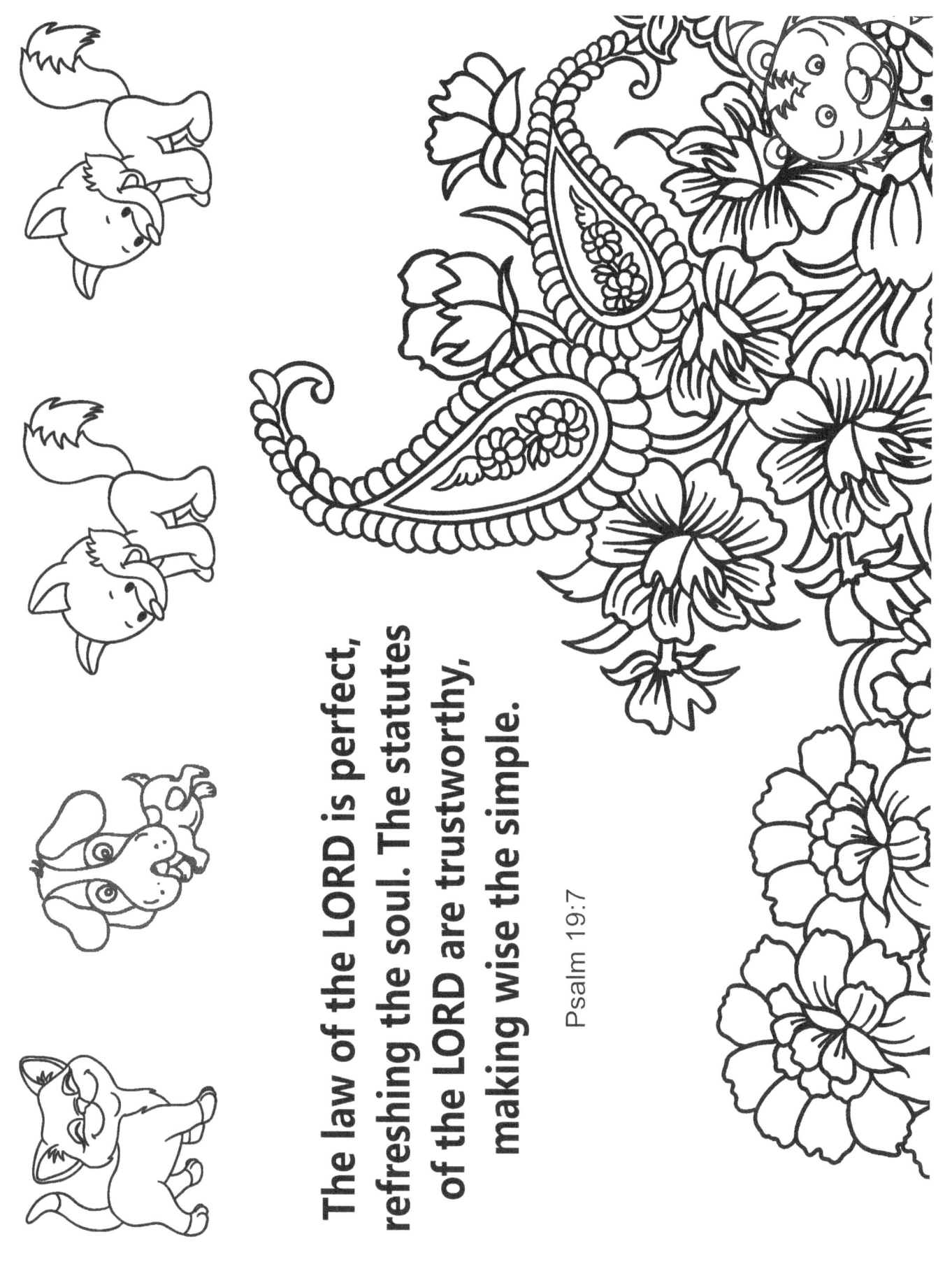

The law of the LORD is perfect, refreshing the soul. The statutes of the LORD are trustworthy, making wise the simple.

Psalm 19:7

The earth is the LORD's, and everything in it, the world, and all who live in it.

Psalm 24:1

The LORD is my light and my salvation – whom shall I fear? The LORD is the stronghold of my life – of whom shall I be afraid?

Psalm 27:1

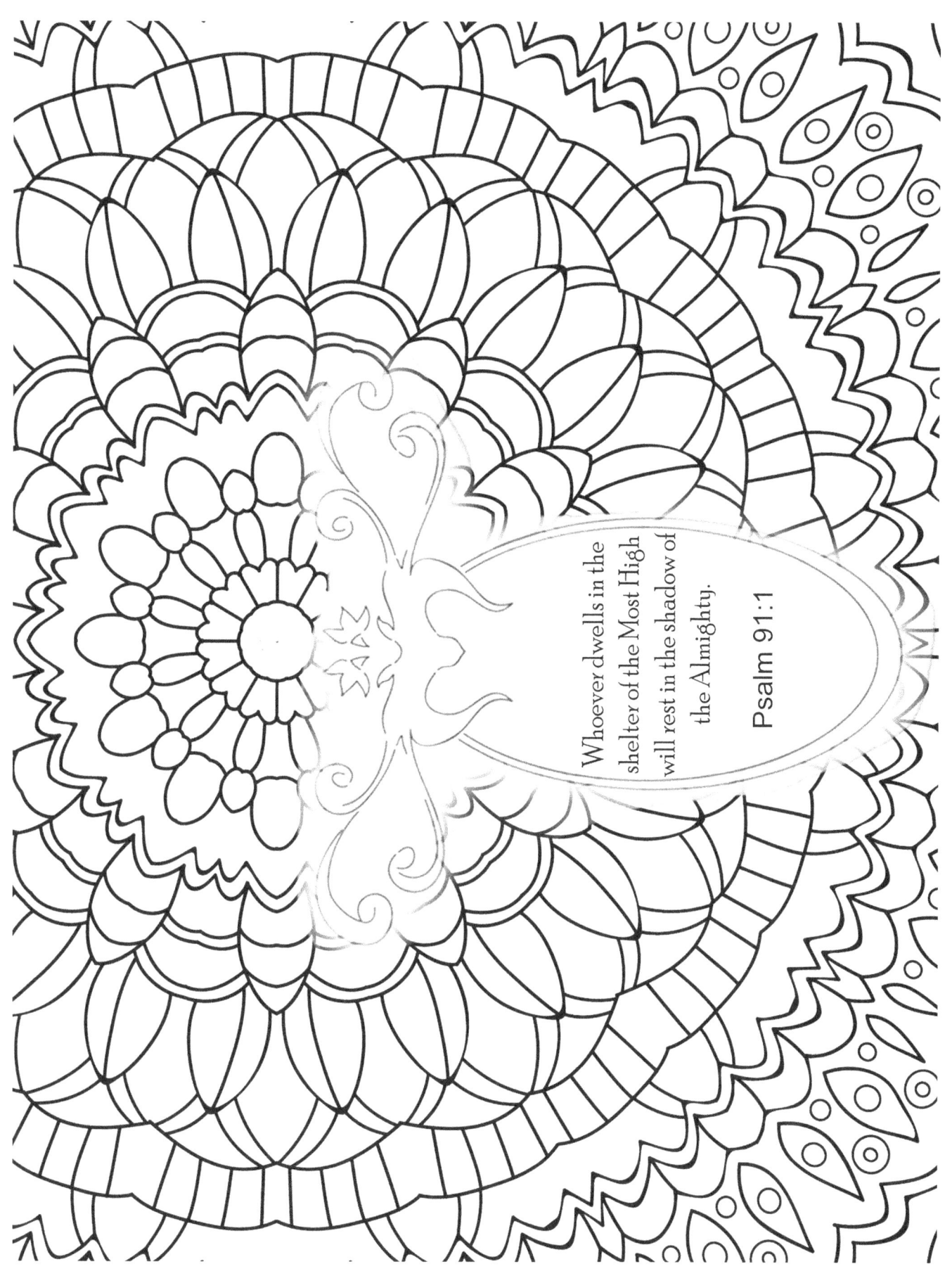

Whoever dwells in the shelter of the Most High will rest in the shadow of the Almighty.

Psalm 91:1

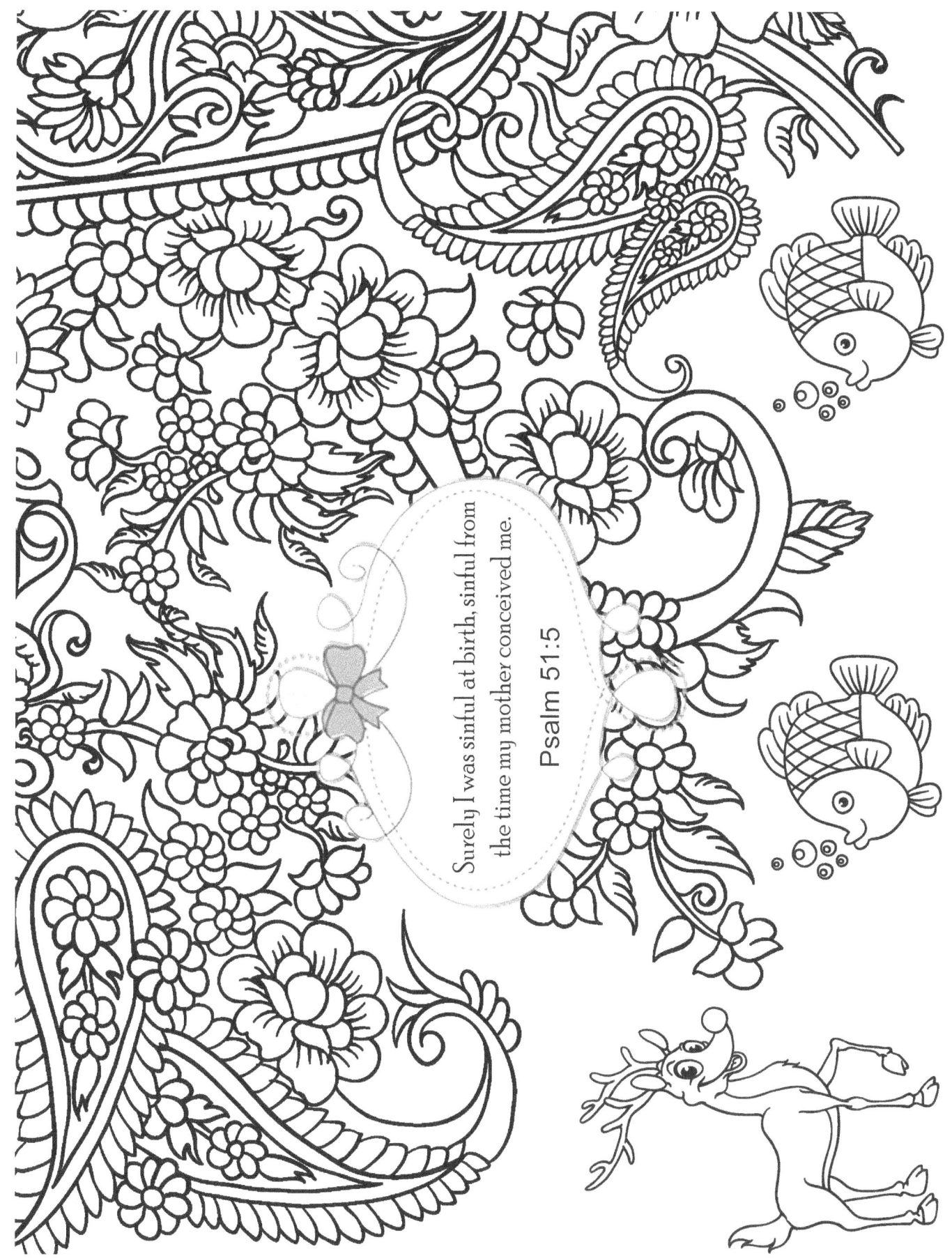

Surely I was sinful at birth, sinful from the time my mother conceived me.

Psalm 51:5

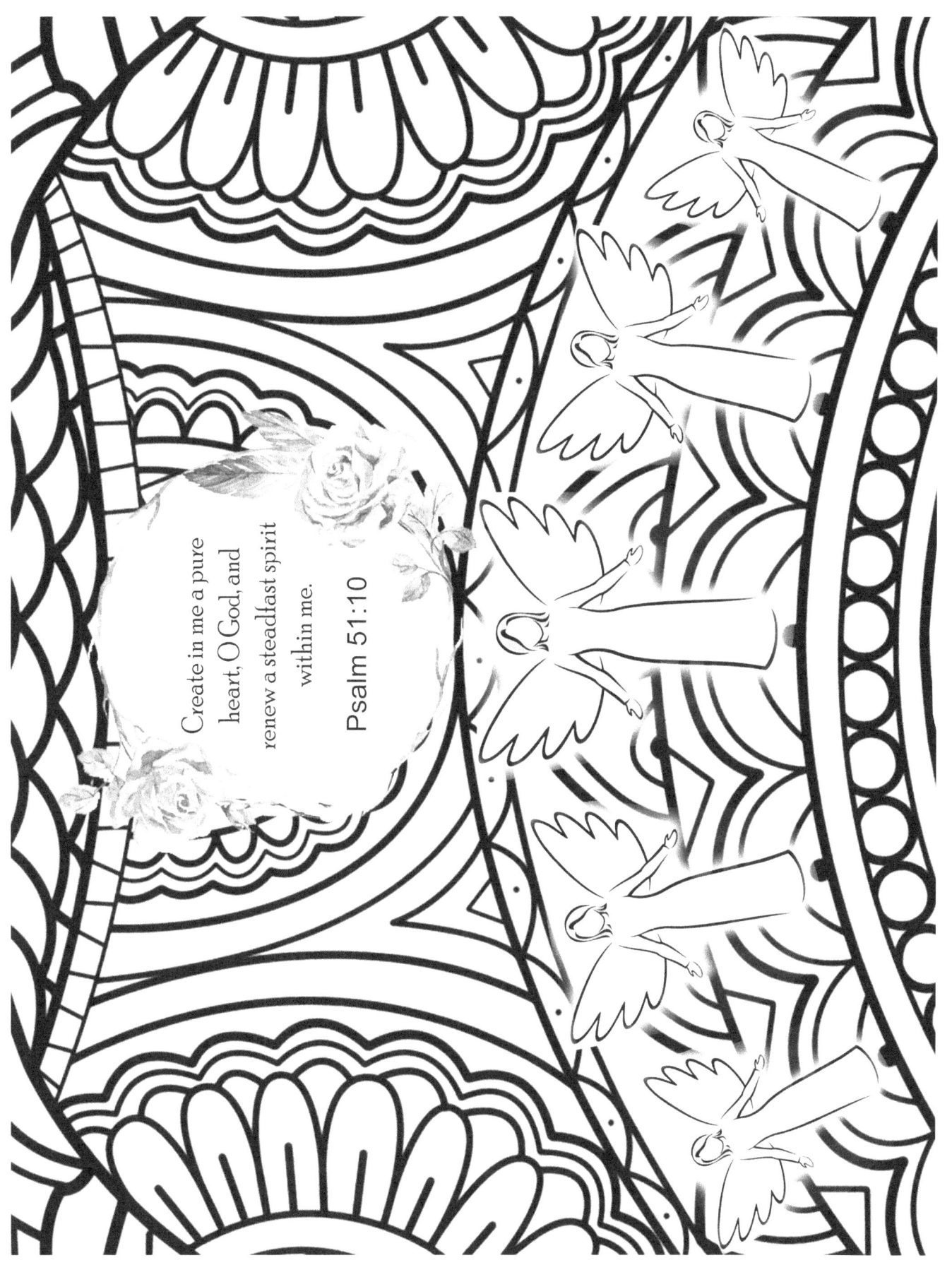

Create in me a pure heart, O God, and renew a steadfast spirit within me.

Psalm 51:10

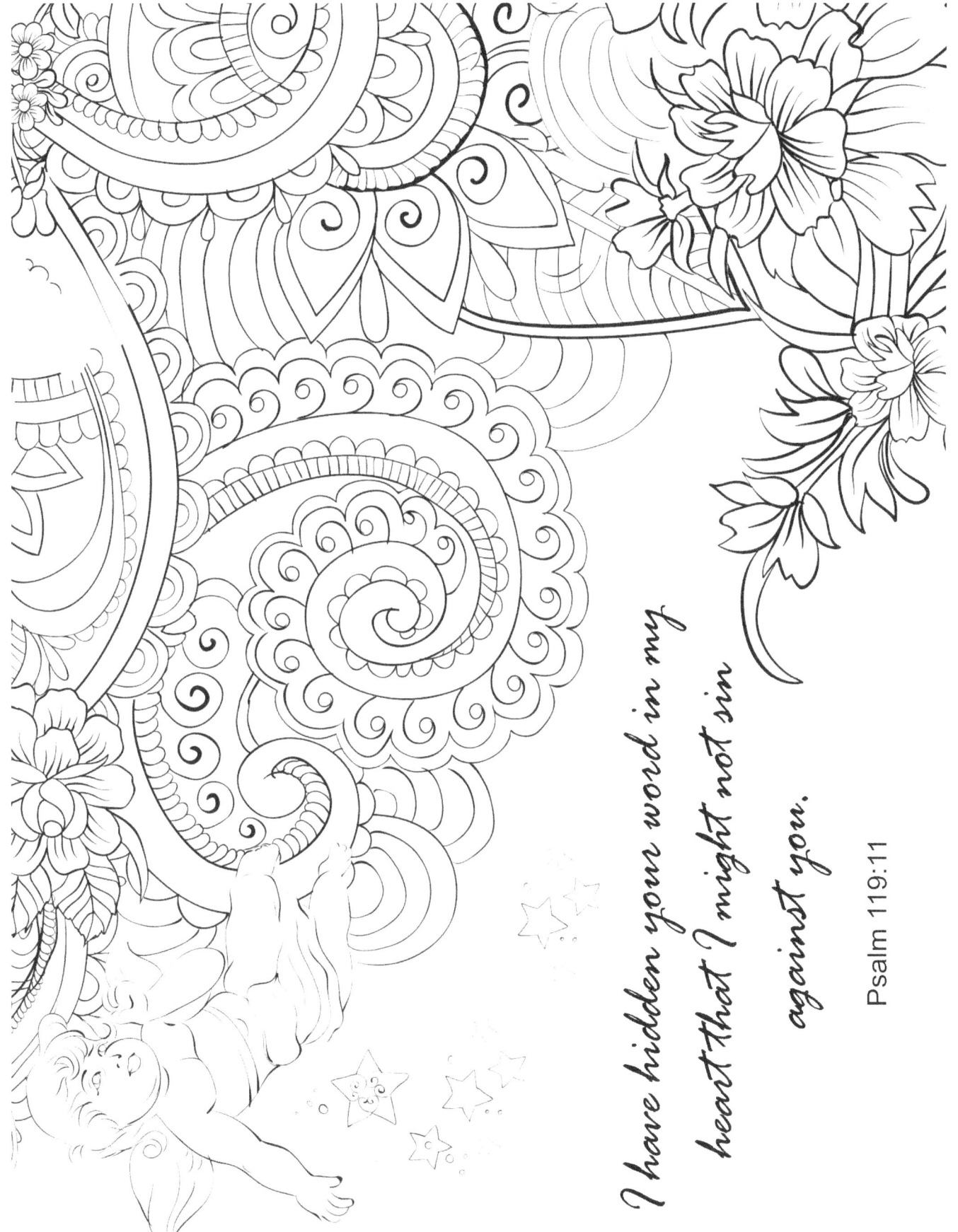

I have hidden your word in my
heart that I might not sin
against you.

Psalm 119:11

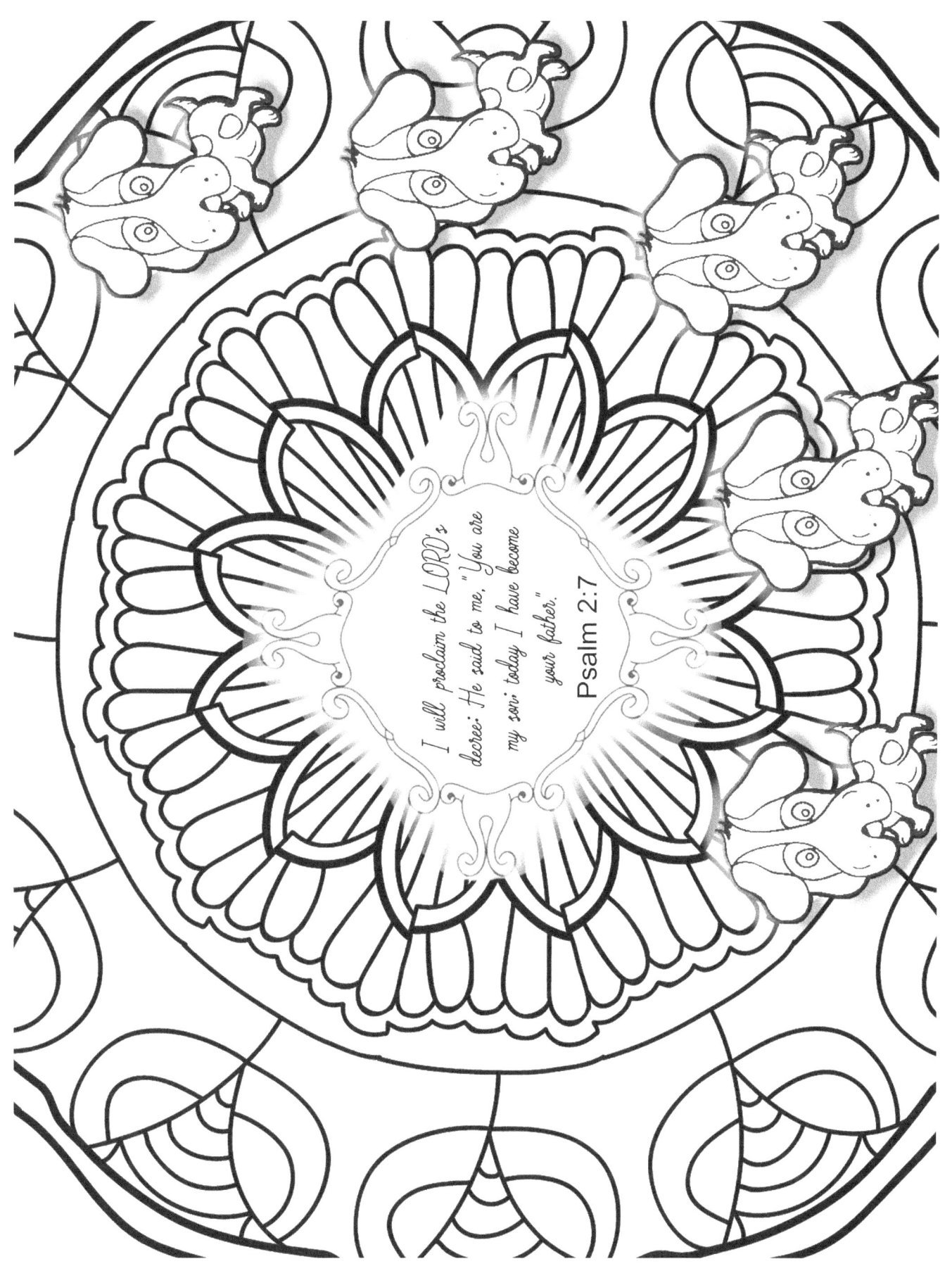

I will proclaim the LORD's decree: He said to me, "You are my son; today I have become your father." Psalm 2:7

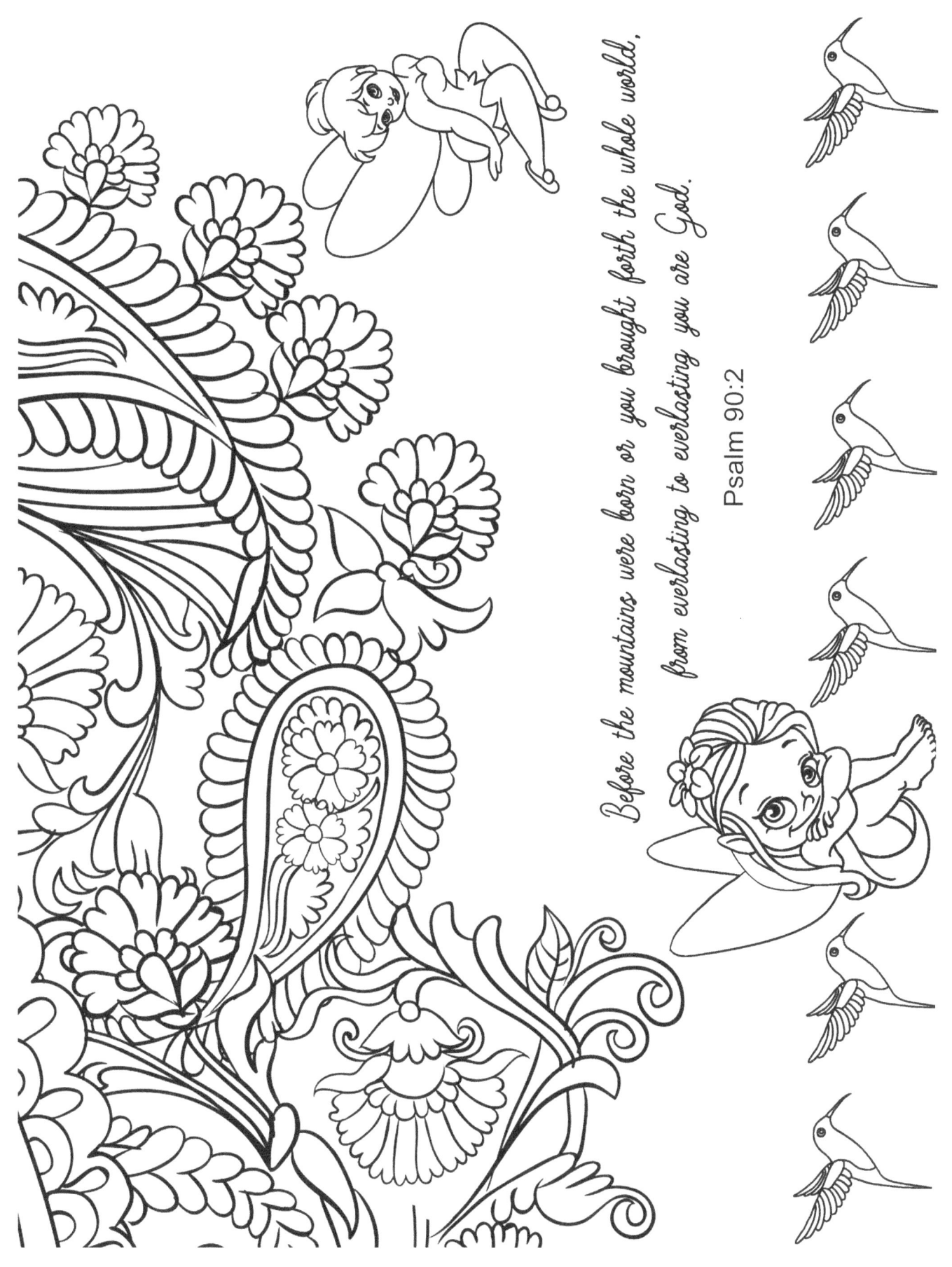

Before the mountains were born or you brought forth the whole world,
from everlasting to everlasting you are God.

Psalm 90:2

I praise you because I am fearfully and wonderfully made; your works are wonderful, I know that full well.

Psalm 139:14

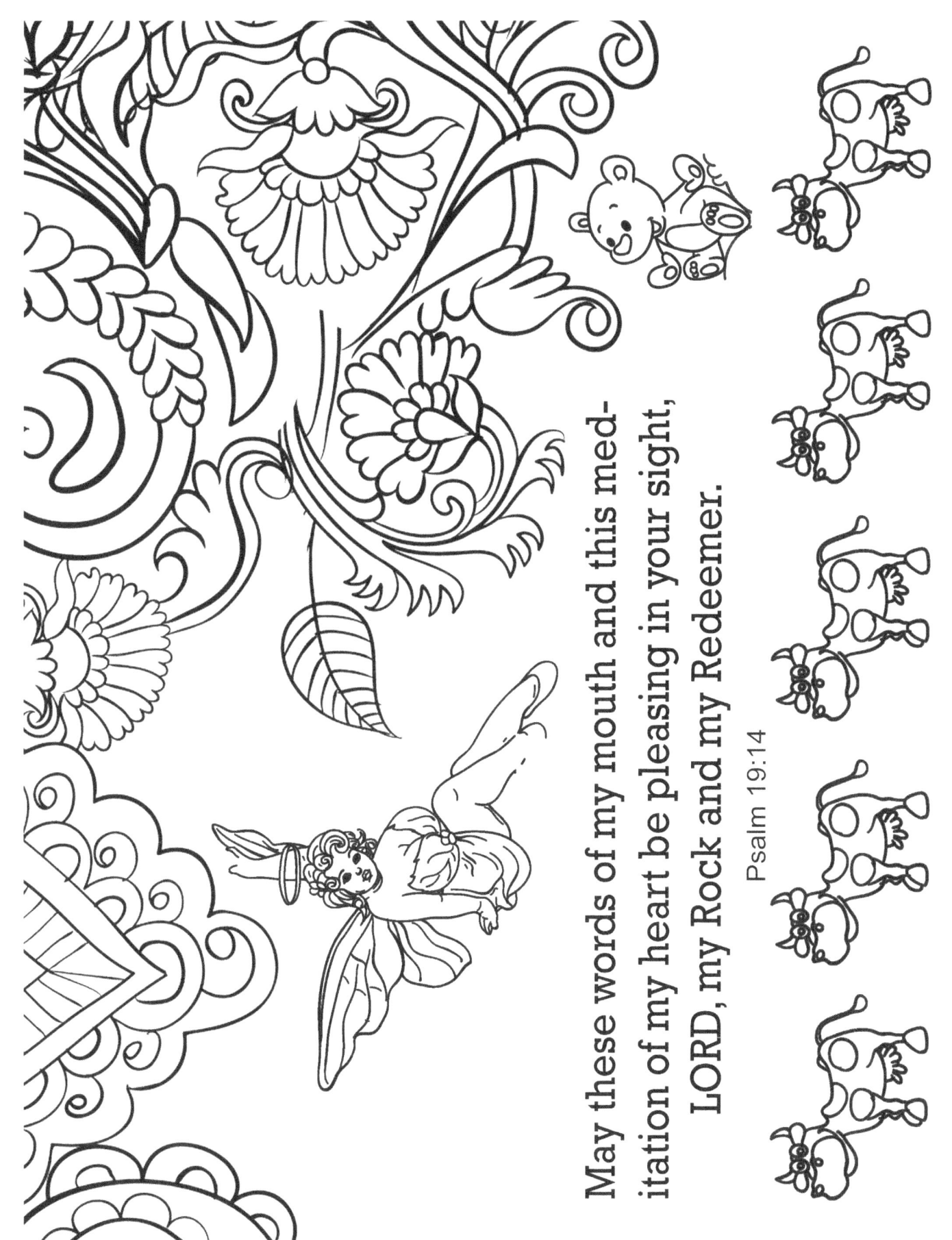

May these words of my mouth and this meditation of my heart be pleasing in your sight, LORD, my Rock and my Redeemer.

Psalm 19:14

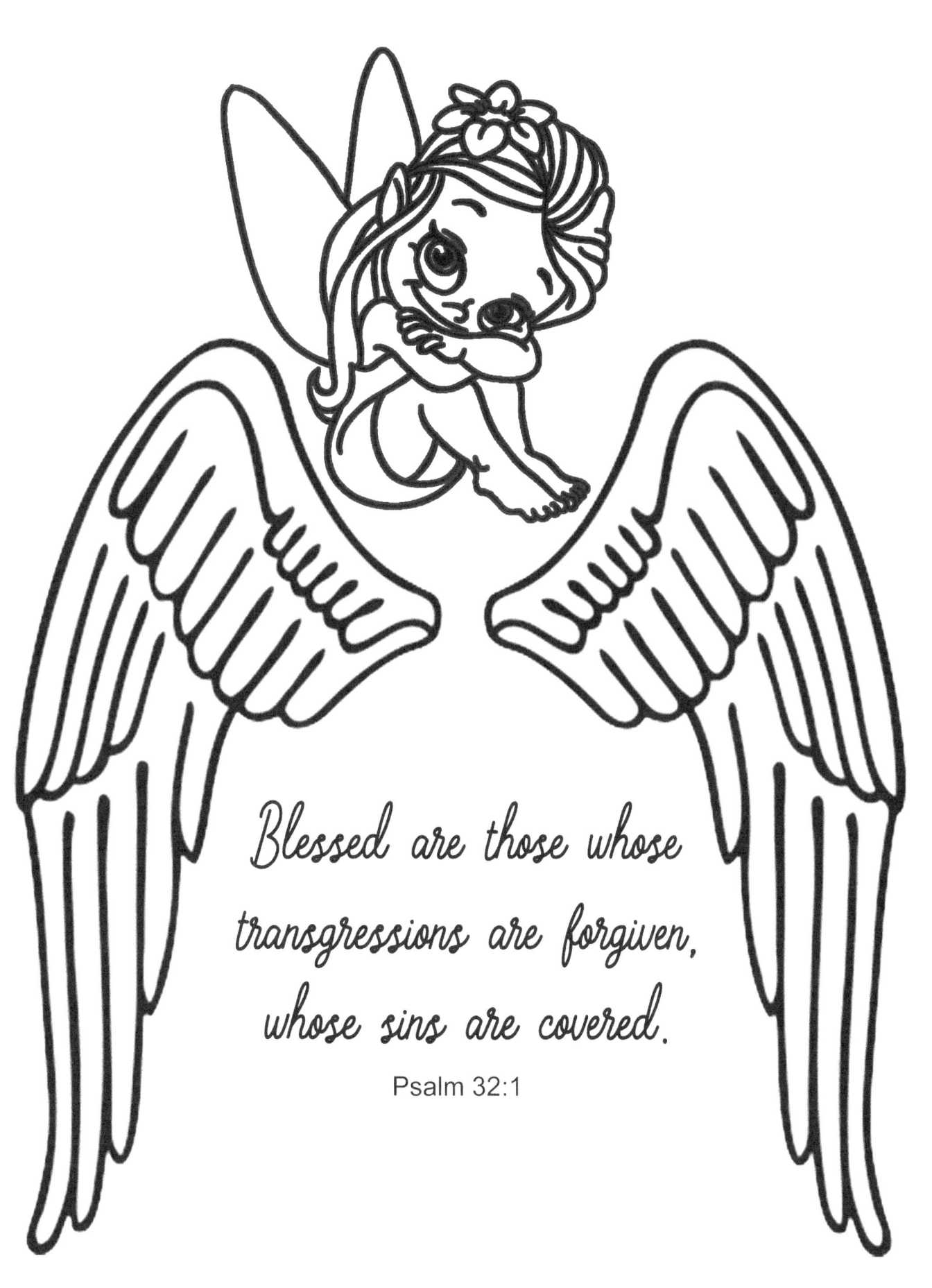

Blessed are those whose transgressions are forgiven, whose sins are covered.

Psalm 32:1